I am the greatest **fighter** in the world. I am the greatest **poet** in the world! I am the greatest! **I am the greatest!**

I'm going to **float like a butterfly, sting like a bee.** Your hands can't hit what your eyes can't see!

God gave me this physical impairment to **remind me** that I'm not the greatest. He is.

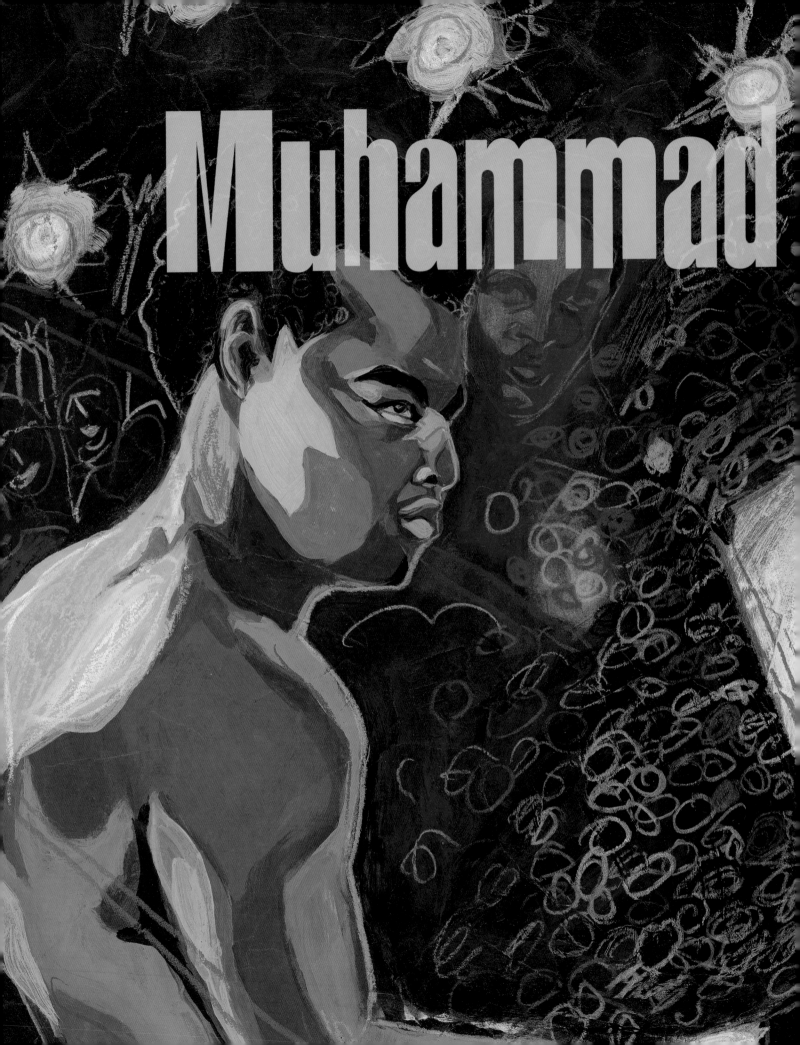

Ali The People's Champion

by Walter Dean Myers
illustrated by Alix Delinois

Collins Amistad

An Imprint of HarperCollinsPublishers

"We called Muhammad 'GG' when he was a baby because he used to say 'gee, gee, gee, gee,'" the champion's mother, Odessa "Bird" Clay, said. "And then, when he became a Golden Gloves champion, he told us he was trying to say 'Golden Gloves.'"

Muhammad Ali was born on the 17th of January, 1942, in Louisville, Kentucky. His parents named him Cassius Marcellus Clay, Jr.

Louisville was a quiet southern town. People rode buses to get around, but a lot of young boys preferred to ride their bicycles.

"One night this kid came downstairs, and he was crying. Somebody had stolen his bicycle, and of course he was very upset about that," Joe Martin, a former policeman, said. "He was only twelve years old then, and he was going to whip whoever stole his bicycle. I said, 'Well, you better learn how to fight before you start challenging people.'"

In his spare time Joe Martin taught kids how to box. Soon, Cassius became a student.

Cassius trained hard in the gym. He didn't hit hard but he could move fast. He also talked a lot about what he was going to do to his opponents.

After fighting in amateur tournaments, Cassius became a Golden Gloves champion.

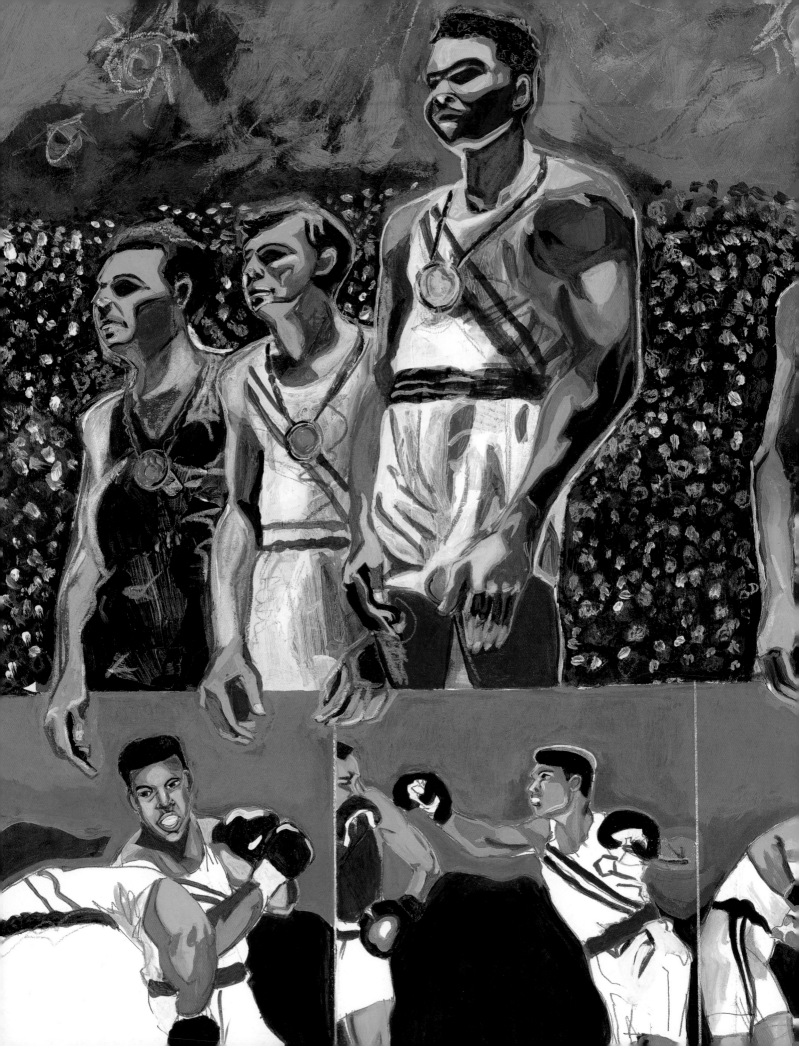

In 1960, at the age of eighteen, he qualified for a place on the American Olympic boxing team. He was on his way to the Games in Rome.

Cassius, who was very fast, won his first fights easily. The fourth fight, for the championship, was much harder.

In the first round, Polish boxer Zbigniew Pietrzykowski used his toughness and experience to push Cassius around. In the second round, Cassius was still losing. But in the third round, the real Cassius Clay emerged. He used all of his skills to outpunch the older man. Cassius Clay, Jr., won the gold. Overnight he became famous all over the world.

And yet, back home there were still many places where black people could not go, even if they had won gold medals in the Olympics.

The Louisville Sponsoring Group took an interest in Cassius and arranged for him to train with an ex-light-heavyweight champ, Archie Moore. But Moore's way of fighting was too defensive for Cassius. He wanted to focus on his speed and fancy footwork. He switched trainers.

In his first professional fight, Cassius defeated Tunney Hunsaker. Over the next three

But many fight fans had doubts. They said Cassius used his speed too much and held his hands too low. And he didn't sound like a heavyweight fighter. "I am the greatest fighter in the world. I am the greatest poet in the world! I am the greatest! I am the greatest!" he shouted. People began calling Cassius the "Louisville Lip."

Cassius loved to get attention and clown around. But he also had a serious side that few people saw. "In Kentucky, black people couldn't ride in the front of a bus," he said, "or drink a cup of coffee where they wanted." Cassius saw people being beaten and put in jail when they tried to get their civil rights.

CLAY
AKA
THE LOUISVILLE LIP

Most people thought Cassius was a loudmouthed young man who had not faced the top fighters. When he signed a contract to fight Charles "Sonny" Liston, the heavyweight champion of the world, one sportswriter wrote, "Some of us would like to buy a large insurance policy on Cassius Clay before he steps in with good old Sonny Liston."

CONVENTION HALL

EVENT

S

LISTON
AKA
THE BLACK BEAR

Liston was a ferocious puncher. He had won his last three fights by knocking out his opponent in the first round. But Cassius was still confident. "I'm going to put that ugly bear on the floor," he said about Sonny Liston. "He's too ugly to be the world champ. The world's champ should be pretty like me!"

"I'm going to float like a butterfly, sting like a bee," Cassius said to anyone who would listen. "Your hands can't hit what your eyes can't see!"

The fight started. Liston, in a rage, threw furious punches at Cassius but kept missing. Cassius hit Liston with quick, stinging punches. Six rounds later, a battered and frustrated Liston did not come out for the seventh round.

Cassius Clay was the heavyweight champion of the world.

THERE IS
NO GOD BUT
ALLAH

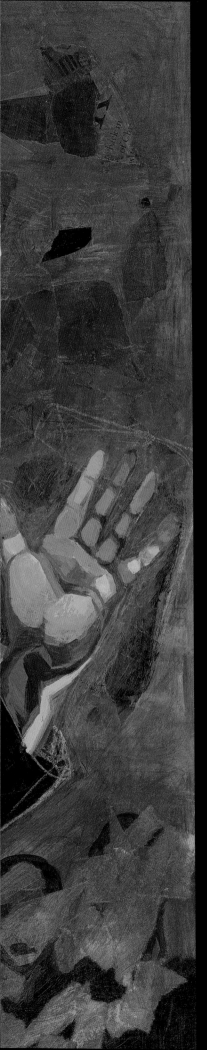

The entire sports world was stunned. Within days Cassius Clay would shock the sports world again. He announced that he had changed his religion and had changed his name. "My name is Muhammad Ali, and I don't want anyone calling me by my slave name, Cassius Clay."

People asked Ali why he had joined the Nation of Islam, a group that many felt wasn't a religious organization but a hate group.

"I choose to be a Muslim. I choose to be a follower of Elijah Muhammad," Ali said, "because he was the only one offering a definite plan which helped my people."

He was asked if he was against white people. He said no. "I like white people. I like my own people," Ali said. "I am America. I am the part you won't recognize. But get used to me. Black, confident, cocky; my name, not yours; my religion, not yours; my goals, my own; get used to me."

Ali hoped that black people would come together and love one another and themselves. Now that he was the heavyweight champion of the world, he thought he should speak out for black people. He said, "I'm not happy riding in a Rolls-Royce, living up on a hill, knowing that my brothers and sisters are down and hungry in a soup line."

It was 1967. The United States was fighting a war in Vietnam. The North Vietnamese said that they were not the enemy of black people.

"Your genuine struggle is on your native land. Go home now, and alive!" they said.

American males had to register for the draft. Ali registered, but when he was called to serve he said, "As a minister of the religion of Islam, I refuse to be inducted into the armed forces of the United States." Many other young men had refused to enter the army or refused to fight because of their religious beliefs. They were called conscientious objectors.

A judge ruled that Ali's reasons for being a conscientious objector were legitimate. But he was still called up to serve. On April 28, 1967, Ali refused to be inducted into the army.

He was sentenced to five years in jail, and his heavyweight championship was taken away. Many people thought the sentence was unfair, and Ali's lawyers appealed to higher courts for justice.

Ali, no longer allowed to fight, spent much of his time as a public speaker. He spoke at colleges around the country and at meetings of the Nation of Islam. He especially liked talking to children. Many people considered him the People's Champion.

Ali was young and good-looking. He gave special meaning to the words "black is beautiful." Ali knew that if he lost his appeals, he would have to go to jail. If he changed his mind and joined the army, he would fight exhibitions and have an easy life, but he decided to follow his convictions. "The man who is not courageous enough to take risks will accomplish nothing in life," he said.

While Ali was waiting to see how his appeal would turn out, more and more people were objecting to the war in Vietnam. The civil rights movement had also grown. Ali's attitudes seemed easier to understand. In October 1970, he was finally allowed to fight again. He won his return match against Jerry Quarry.

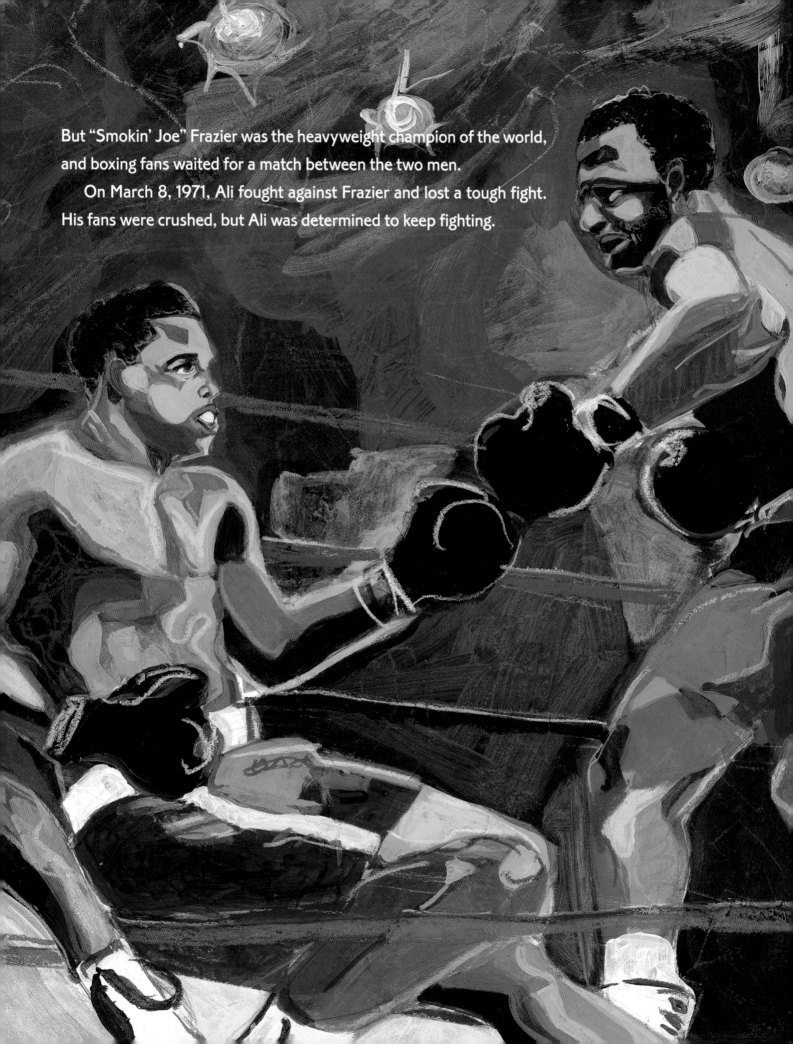

But "Smokin' Joe" Frazier was the heavyweight champion of the world, and boxing fans waited for a match between the two men.

On March 8, 1971, Ali fought against Frazier and lost a tough fight. His fans were crushed, but Ali was determined to keep fighting.

On June 28, 1971, the Supreme Court of the United States ruled that Ali should have been excused from serving in the army. Ali, the fighter in the ring, had won an important fight in the Supreme Court.

"I never thought of myself as great when I refused to go in the army," Ali said. "All I did was stand up for what I believed. I wanted America to be America. And now the whole world knows that."

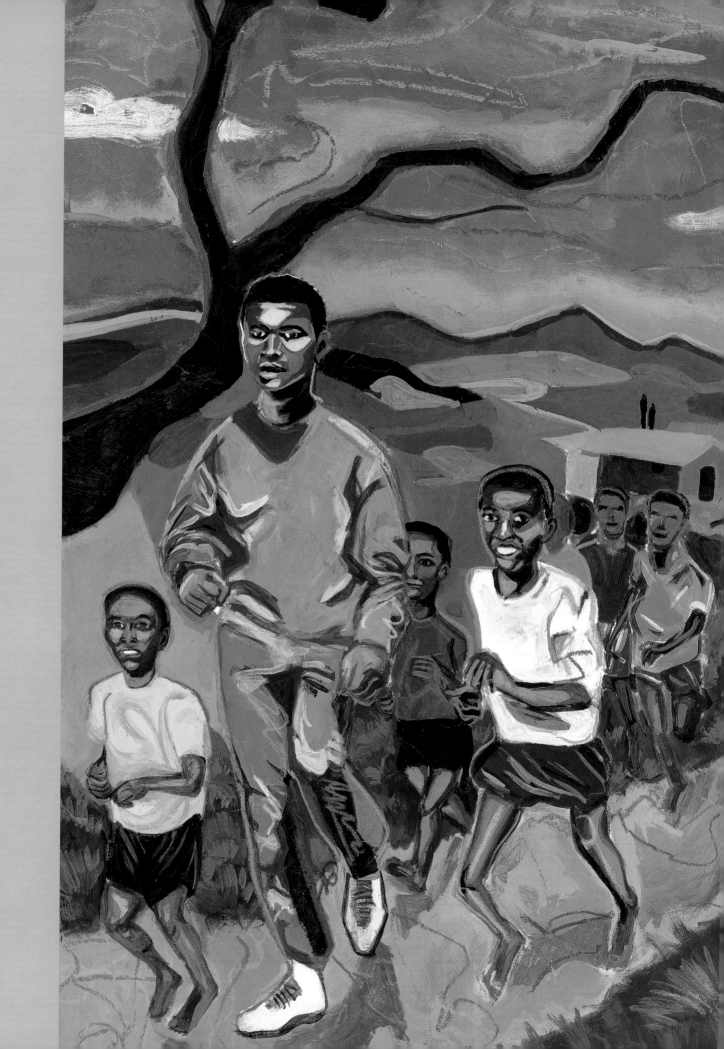

Ali was the most entertaining fighter in the history of the sport. He fought every major fighter of his time. One of his toughest fights was known as the Rumble in the Jungle. He was going to fight George Foreman in Zaire, in central Africa. Foreman was the new heavyweight champion. Ali, now thirty-two, was expected to lose to the younger fighter. But Ali had a different idea. "Now you see me, now you don't, George thinks he will, but I know he won't."

When the fight started, the African crowd, which was in favor of Ali, shouted, *"Ali Bamba ye!"* over and over again. Foreman wasn't bothered. He came forward and caught Ali against the ropes. Over and over his massive arms swung at Ali. Ali's trainers yelled at him to get away from the ropes.

Ali allowed Foreman to punch away under the hot lights. He called his plan of laying against the ropes the "rope-a-dope."

"I lay on the ropes and said, 'Punch, sucker. I thought you could hit. That's a sissy punch.'"

In the eighth round, Foreman tired, and Ali saw his chance. Ali's punches were fast and hard. Big George Foreman was stunned, then hurt. He stumbled toward the canvas, and the referee started counting over him. Ali was once again the champion of the world.

Ali fought for seven more years after the Rumble in the Jungle. He finally retired in 1981 at the age of thirty-nine. His fighting career was over, and now he was facing yet another tough opponent, a nerve disorder called Parkinson's disease.

"God gave me this physical impairment to remind me that I'm not the greatest," Ali said. "He is."

In 1996, Ali was asked to light the Olympic torch at the Games in Atlanta, Georgia. As he lifted the flame to light the torch, the world could see that he was still, within himself, a fighter and would continue fighting the disease. Millions of people around the world cheered him. Muhammad Ali was, indeed, the People's Champion.

To Alex and Elveus Delinois and Anita Kover
—A.D.

January 17, 1942	Cassius Marcellus Clay, Jr., is born: Louisville, KY
September 5, 1960	Is awarded Olympic gold medal, light-heavyweight division, 1960 Summer Olympic Games: Rome, Italy
October 29, 1960	Wins first professional fight against Tunney Hunsaker: Louisville, KY
February 25, 1964	Beats Sonny Liston to win world heavyweight title: Miami Beach, FL
February 26, 1964	Converts to Muslim religion
March 6, 1964	Takes the name Muhammad Ali
April 28, 1967	Refuses to be inducted into the U.S. armed forces
June 27, 1967	Is stripped of boxing title and banned from the sport
October 26, 1970	Wins return match against Jerry Quarry: Atlanta, GA
March 8, 1971	Loses to Joe Frazier, world heavyweight champion: New York, NY
June 28, 1971	Has conviction on refusing to be inducted into the armed forces reversed by U.S. Supreme Court
October 30, 1974	Wins Rumble in the Jungle against George Foreman: Kinshasa, Zaire
October 1, 1975	Wins Thrilla in Manila against Joe Frazier: Quezon City, Philippines
December 11, 1981	Loses to Trevor Berbick in his last fight: Nassau, Bahamas
July 19, 1996	Lights Olympic torch, Summer Olympic Games: Atlanta, GA
1998–present	Serves as a United Nations Messenger of Peace
December 2, 1999	Is named Sportsman of the Century by *Sports Illustrated*
November 9, 2005	Is awarded Presidential Medal of Freedom

Muhammad Ali: The People's Champion
Collins and Amistad are imprints of HarperCollins Publishers.
Text copyright © 2010 by Walter Dean Myers Illustrations copyright © 2010 by Alix Delinois Manufactured in China. All rights reserved. No part of this book may be used or reproduced in any manner whatsoever without written permission except in the case of brief quotations embodied in critical articles and reviews. For information address HarperCollins Children's Books, a division of HarperCollins Publishers, 10 East 53rd Street, New York, NY 10022. www.harpercollinschildrens.com Library of Congress Cataloging-in-Publication Data is available. ISBN 978-0-06-029131-0 (trade bdg.) — ISBN 978-0-06-029132-7 (lib. bdg.)
Design by Stephanie Bart-Horvath 10 11 12 13 14 LEO 10 9 8 7 6 5 4 3 2 1 ❖ First Edition